# RECORD-BREAKING DINOSAUR FACTS

And the SCIENCE behind them!

IZZI HOWELL

WAYLAND

First published in Great Britain in 2026
by Hodder & Stoughton
Copyright © Hodder & Stoughton, 2026
Produced for Wayland by

All rights reserved.

Editor: Izzi Howell
Designer: Clare Nicholas

HB ISBN: 978 1 5263 2969 1
PB ISBN: 978 1 5263 2970 7

Wayland
An imprint of
Hachette Children's Group
Part of Hodder & Stoughton
Carmelite House
50 Victoria Embankment
London EC4Y 0DZ

An Hachette UK Company
www.hachette.co.uk
www.hachettechildrens.co.uk

The authorised representative in the EEA is Hachette Ireland, 8 Castlecourt Centre, Dublin 15, D15 XTP3, Ireland (email: info@hbgi.ie)

Printed in Dubai

Picture acknowledgements:
Shutterstock: Catmando, Hakim Graphy, blueinthesky, Pedro Moraes, Sebastian Kaulitzki, Warpaint, Daniel Eskridge and Herschel Hoffmeyer cover, Warpaint 3t, 8-9 and 12-13, Catmando 3b, 4l, 10-11, 14-15, 22-23 and 23t, Elenarts 4r, 16-17 and 21t, Warpaint 5tl, Hakim Graphy 5tr and 29b, Romolo Tavani 5b, Herschel Hoffmeyer 6-7, 7b, 9b and 28t, oldshen 7t, Aryasakti 9t and 17t, lady-luck 11l, Daniel Eskridge 11r, 18-19, 24-25, 30t and 31, Antonov Maxim 12b, IanC66 13t, Nuntiya 13b, William Cushman 15t, MaryValery 15b, Abdul_Shakoor 17b, AKKHARAT JARUSILAWONG 19t, HitToon 19b, Sebastian Kaulitzki 20-21, Handies Peak and Alex Darts 21b, Maquiladora 23c, Jaroslav Moravcik 23b, Marti Bug Catcher 25t, Katarzyna Lukasik 25b, Pedro Moraes 26-27, Adwo 27t and 30b, LukaSkywalker 27b, Nicholas Courtney 28b; Wikimedia: Sereno et al 14b, Lucas-Attwell 28c, Gary Todd 29c. All design elements from Shutterstock.

The website addresses (URLs) included in this book were valid at the time of going to press. However, it is possible that contents or addresses may have changed since the publication of this book. No responsibility for any such changes can be accepted by either the author or the publisher.

All facts and statistics were correct at the time of press.

# MEASUREMENTS

Keep track of all the measurements in the book with this handy guide!

cm = centimetre
m = metre
km = kilometre
g = gram
kg = kilogram
N = newton

# CONTENTS

| | |
|---|---|
| Diverse dinos | 4 |
| Bone-crushing bite | 6 |
| Baby brain | 8 |
| Claw-some lengths | 10 |
| Small-o-saurus | 12 |
| Too many teeth? | 14 |
| Number one dino | 16 |
| Sturdy skulls | 18 |
| Tail titan | 20 |
| Mum's the word | 22 |
| Crest champion | 24 |
| Bonkers big | 26 |
| More incredible dinosaur records | 28 |
| Glossary | 30 |
| Further information | 31 |
| Index | 32 |

Check me out on page 10!

# DIVERSE DINOS

**MOST DIVERSE TIME PERIOD**

Dinosaurs walked on Earth for around 170 million years. During that time, they evolved into many different species in all shapes and sizes. However, it was during the **CRETACEOUS PERIOD** that dinosaur diversity was at its peak.

## TRIASSIC PERIOD
(252 to 201 million years ago)

## JURASSIC PERIOD
(201 to 145 million years ago)

*Coelophysis*

The first dinosaurs evolved from prehistoric reptiles called archosaurs during the Triassic Period, around 240 million years ago.

As the Triassic Period went on, these early dinosaurs evolved into new types of dinosaur, including fierce theropods and large sauropods.

Many large archosaurs became extinct at the end of the Triassic Period. Dinosaurs grew to dominate Earth throughout the Jurassic Period.

*Megalosaurus*

4

# Cretaceous Period
## (145 to 66 million years ago)

*Stegosaurus*

By the Cretaceous Period, dinosaurs had ruled our planet for millions of years. With so much time to evolve, they were able to diversify into many different species, suited to every habitat and position in the food chain.

More diverse species of theropod and sauropod appeared in the Jurassic Period, along with early stegosaurs and ankylosaurs.

*Spinosaurus*

At the end of the Cretaceous Period, a massive asteroid crashed into Earth. Scientists believe that the impact created so much dust that it blocked heat from the Sun, making our planet suddenly much colder and darker. Many animals and plants struggled to survive as a result and huge numbers of species, including the dinosaurs, became extinct.

# BONE-CRUSHING BITE

**MOST POWERFUL BITE**

**TYRANNOSAURUS REX'S** reputation as a fearsome predator was well deserved. It boasted the most powerful bite of any land animal *ever*, measuring three and a half times stronger than that of a saltwater crocodile, which has the strongest bite of any living animal.

## MEASURING BITES

An animal's bite is measured in newtons (N), which is a unit of force. A human can bite with a force of around 285 N. *T. rex's* bite is estimated to have reached a whopping 57,000 N!

*T. rex* combined its powerful bite with a mouthful of up to 60 sharp teeth, some measuring up to 15 cm long. The force of its jaw muscles allowed its teeth to crunch through bone.

Palaeontologists have identified spaces in *T. rex*'s jaw for mega jaw-closing muscles, which provided the force behind its mighty bite.

As *T. rex*'s small front legs weren't big enough to grab or attack, it probably used its strong bite to grip its prey instead.

# DID YOU KNOW?

The amount of force generated by the bite of an adult *T. rex* was equivalent to the weight of three small cars pressing down!

# BORN TO BITE?

*T. rex* wasn't born with a bone-crushing bite. A young *T. rex* would have had a much weaker bite (only around as strong as that of a lion!) and so probably hunted smaller animals. As its jaws grew larger and more muscular, its biting power increased.

*T. rex* used its powerful bite and strong muscles in its neck to rip meat off its prey.

# BABY BRAIN

**SMALLEST BRAIN BY SIZE**

Despite reaching lengths of around 9 m, *STEGOSAURUS'* brain was the size of a plum! This gives it the slightly undesirable title of smallest dinosaur brain in proportion to its body.

There is much debate over the purpose of *Stegosaurus*' plates. They may have been used to help *Stegosaurus* recognise each other, attract a mate or possibly to help them control their body temperature.

In the past, some scientists were so puzzled by the tiny size of *Stegosaurus*' brain that they suggested it may have had an extra brain in a space near its hips! However, there's no evidence that this was the case.

# BIGGER BODIES, BIGGER BRAINS?

*Stegosaurus* wasn't the only dinosaur with a teeny tiny brain. Many dinosaurs had surprisingly small brains compared to their overall size. However, that doesn't mean that they weren't intelligent. Scientists have discovered that once animals evolve to reach a certain size, their brains don't continue to increase in size at the same rate as their body.

## DID YOU KNOW?

The empty space near *Stegosaurus*' hips probably contained energy stores that it could use for an extra boost!

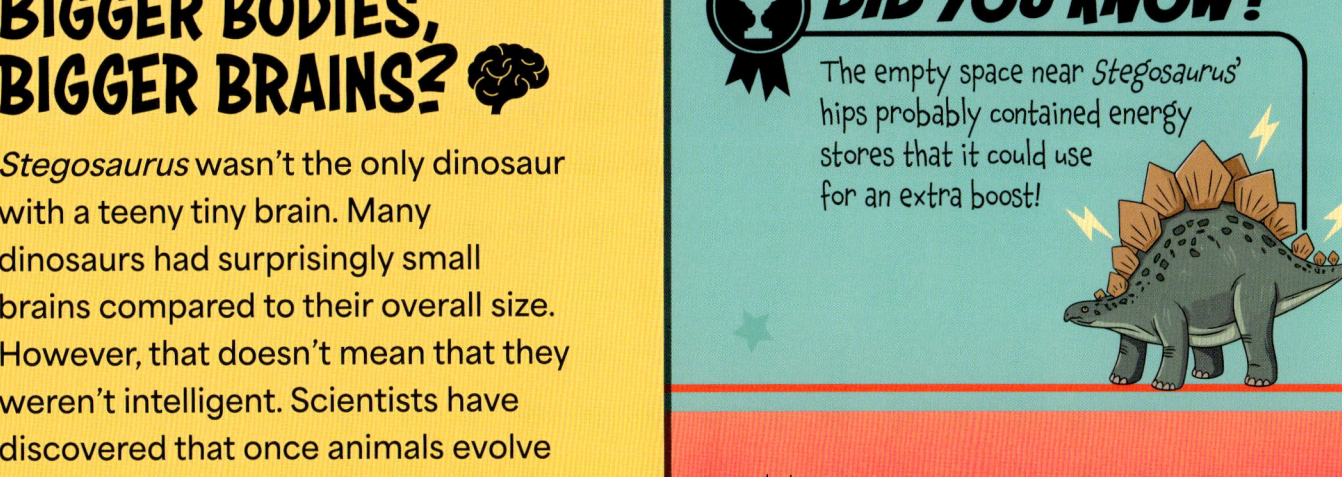

## SMART BUT SMALL

Small brains can also be packed with brilliant brain cells that boost an animal's intelligence. For example, certain brainy birds, such as crows, have much smaller brains than clever primates, but they have around the same number of brain cells, because theirs are packed much closer together. It's possible that dinosaur brains may have also had a similar structure.

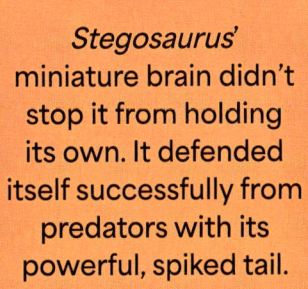

*Stegosaurus*' miniature brain didn't stop it from holding its own. It defended itself successfully from predators with its powerful, spiked tail.

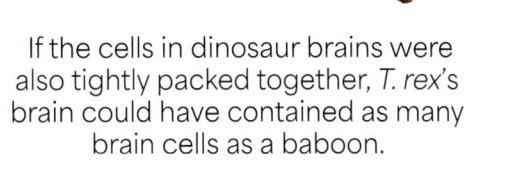

If the cells in dinosaur brains were also tightly packed together, *T. rex*'s brain could have contained as many brain cells as a baboon.

# CLAW-SOME LENGTHS

**LONGEST CLAWS**

Watch out! **THERIZINOSAURUS** had giant, curved claws that nearly reached 1 m in length! The good news is that although *Therizinosaurus'* claws look like deadly weapons, they were actually used for much more innocent purposes.

Even though *Therizinosaurus* belonged to the typically carnivorous theropod family, palaeontologists know from its teeth that it was actually a herbivore. It used its massive claws to defend itself against predators and to grab plants to eat.

Other members of the therizinosaur family had smaller claws adapted for digging and hooking. Palaeontologists believe that it's possible that other theropods, such as *Velociraptor*, may have also used their claws for other tasks, other than just attacking!

# CLAW CALCULATIONS

When it comes to claw length, *Therizinosaurus* is number one. However, scientists often look at the ratio between claw length and body length instead. It's hardly surprising that big animals have big claws ... what's more impressive is when animals have particularly long claws when compared to their overall size.

## THE REAL CHAMPION

Unfortunately, a complete *Therizinosaurus* skeleton has never been found, so scientists can only estimate its size. They believe that *Therizinosaurus* was probably about 10-12 m long, which means that its claws were around 10 per cent of its overall length. The modern giant armadillo's claws are much smaller than *Therizinosaurus*' at just 20 cm long, but make up a record-breaking 22 per cent of its overall length.

*Therizinosaurus* needed a large digestive system to help it break down its diet of plants. As a result, it ended up with a bit of a pot belly!

*Therizinosaurus*' height allowed it to nibble on tasty branches that smaller herbivores couldn't reach.

## DID YOU KNOW?

When first discovered, palaeontologists believed *Therizinosaurus* fossils to be the bones of a giant turtle!

Seriously?!

# SMALL-O-SAURUS

**SMALLEST DINOSAUR**

We often think of dinosaurs as towering giants, but they actually came in all shapes and sizes. The dinkiest dinosaur was **MICRORAPTOR** at just 77 cm long - about the size of a modern crow!

## BIRD OR DINOSAUR?

*Microraptor* belonged to the theropod family of dinosaurs, along with *T. rex* and *Velociraptor*. Some theropods evolved into the first birds and are the ancestors of the birds that live today. However, *Microraptor* lived alongside early birds and so wasn't a direct relation. Their similarity to birds is an example of convergent evolution - when two species develop the same traits independently of each other.

Palaeontologists have discovered tiny, preserved pigment cells in fossilised *Microraptor* feathers. These pigments suggest that *Microraptor*'s feathers were black and shiny.

## DID YOU KNOW?

*Microraptor* fossils are found very frequently by palaeontologists, which suggests that they were probably a very common dinosaur in the Cretaceous Period.

*Not another Microraptor!*

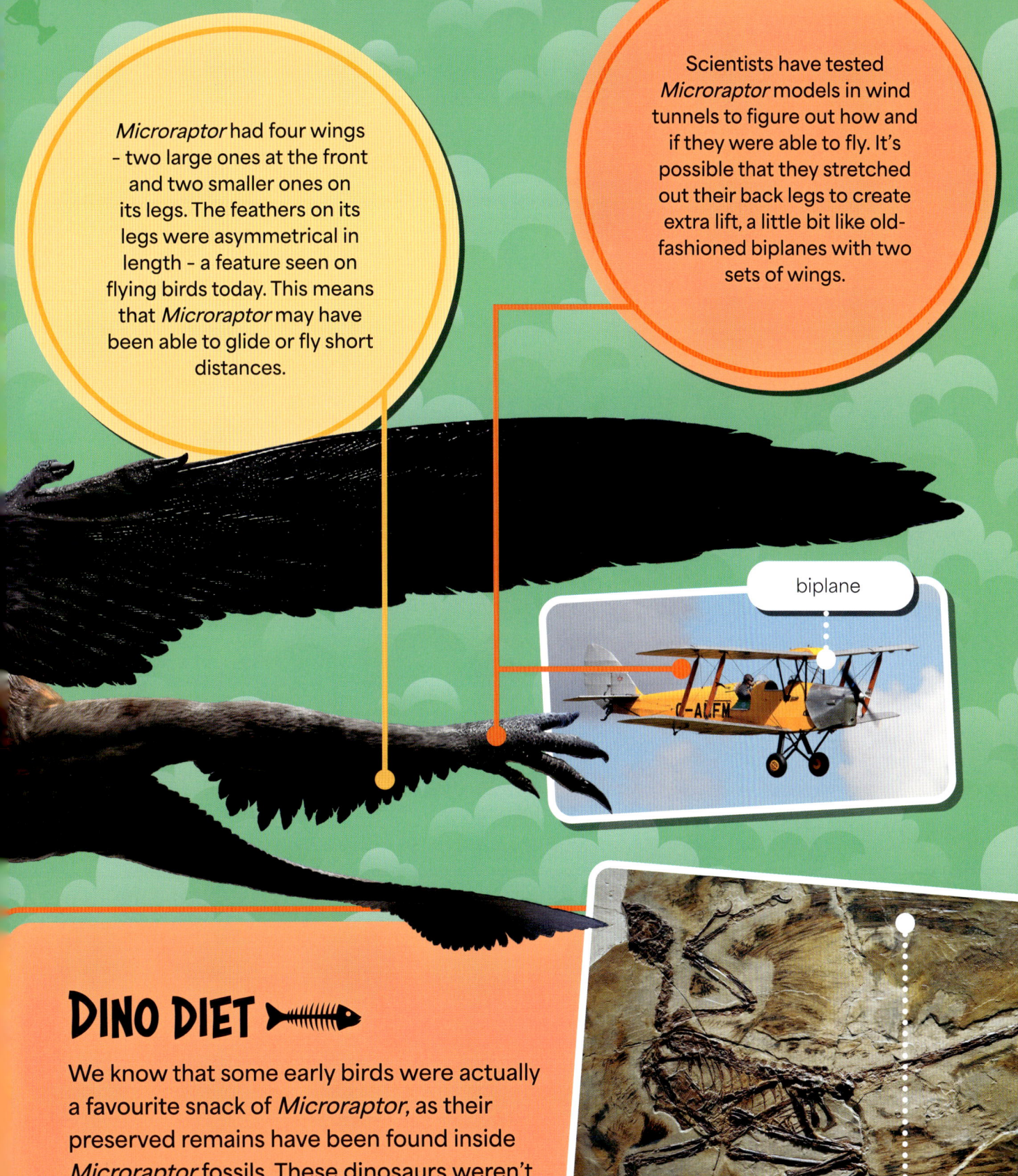

*Microraptor* had four wings - two large ones at the front and two smaller ones on its legs. The feathers on its legs were asymmetrical in length - a feature seen on flying birds today. This means that *Microraptor* may have been able to glide or fly short distances.

Scientists have tested *Microraptor* models in wind tunnels to figure out how and if they were able to fly. It's possible that they stretched out their back legs to create extra lift, a little bit like old-fashioned biplanes with two sets of wings.

biplane

## Dino Diet

We know that some early birds were actually a favourite snack of *Microraptor*, as their preserved remains have been found inside *Microraptor* fossils. These dinosaurs weren't picky eaters, and also enjoyed munching on fish, mammals and small reptiles - pretty much anything that moved!

These black streaks are *Microraptor*'s preserved feathers.

# TOO MANY TEETH?

**MOST TEETH**

**NIGERSAURUS** had over 500 teeth - just imagine its trips to the dentist! Why did this dinosaur need so many teeth?

*Nigersaurus* had a wide, flat mouth. Teeth ran all the way across the front of its top and bottom jaw.

## 🌿 TOUGH LUNCH

*Nigersaurus* was a herbivore that grazed on ferns and other low shrubs. Grazing on these tough plants quickly wore down *Nigersaurus*' teeth, making them much less effective. The solution? Replace the teeth often, every 14 days to be precise!

About 120 teeth were visible in *Nigersaurus*' jaw at any time. The extra 380 or so teeth were stacked vertically in columns inside its jaw.

When one tooth fell out, the next tooth moved into the jaw to take its place!

column of teeth

# BONE BOTHER 🔍

It has been challenging for palaeontologists to study *Nigersaurus* fossils as its skull was extremely thin and delicate, making it hard to preserve and identify. Some connecting bones in the head were less than 2 mm thick!

Despite the difficulty of finding fragile *Nigersaurus* remains, we have been lucky enough to find enough bones to get a good idea of what its skull and teeth would have looked like! This model is based on these remains.

## DID YOU KNOW?

*Nigersaurus* was the only dinosaur with teeth arranged in a totally flat line! Most dinosaurs' teeth curved around their jaws, just like ours do. Can you imagine how weird we'd look with teeth like a *Nigersaurus*?

# NUMBER ONE DINO

**MEGALOSAURUS**, the first dinosaur to be named, got its name before the word 'dinosaur' had even been invented! Let's take a trip back through time to learn more about how the first dinosaurs were identified in the 19th century.

## ANCIENT MYSTERIES

Dinosaur fossils were found many times throughout history. While no one realised what they were at the time, people came up with alternative theories to explain these enormous bones. Some cultures believed them to be dragon bones, while others thought they were the remains of giants or gods.

In the early 19th century, British scientist William Buckland was studying some enormous fossilised bones and teeth. He compared them to the bones and teeth of modern animals and realised that they were similar to those of modern lizards.

Buckland concluded that the bones belonged to a 9-m-long reptile. He named this animal *Megalosaurus*, meaning great lizard. Buckland didn't realise it at the time, but he had just named the first dinosaur!

Over the next decades, the remains of many more prehistoric species were discovered. Scientists started to notice patterns between the fossils, and they started to classify them into different categories. Large reptiles, such as *Megalosaurus*, were grouped together under a new name – 'dinosaurs'.

## DID YOU KNOW?

The name dinosaur comes from the Ancient Greek words *deinos* meaning 'terrible' and *sauros* meaning 'lizard'. Terrible not only refers to the dinosaurs' deadly power, but also their impressive size.

*Who are you calling terrible?!*

## LEARNING MORE

Back in the 19th century, scientists had to make guesses about how dinosaurs looked and behaved based on the limited fossils they had available. Thanks to modern technology and the discovery of many more dinosaur fossils, we now have much stronger evidence to support our theories.

This statue of *Megalosaurus* was built in the 1850s. Back then, scientists believed it was a long, low reptile that walked on four legs. Since then, we've found fossil evidence to suggest it was a leaner predator that stood upright on two legs.

# Sturdy SKULLS

**THICKEST SKULL**

**PACHYCEPHALOSAURUS** had a built-in protective helmet – a 22-cm-thick section of bone at the front of its skull! That's 20 times thicker than normal. But why did *Pachycephalosaurus* need such bulky bone in its head?

## BIG BANGERS

Contrary to popular belief, it's unlikely that *Pachycephalosaurus* head-butted each other directly with their hard, bony domes. However, scientists do believe that they may have used their strong skulls to hit each other on the side during disputes about territory or mating.

The front section of the skull was made out of a special type of bone that contained cells to help repair bone damage. This suggests that fractures from strong whacks were frequent!

The dome on its head was surrounded by short spikes – all the better for hitting with!

The bone at the front of *Pachycephalosaurus*' head was so thick that it could be seen as a large, bony dome from the outside.

# END OF AN ERA

*Pachycephalosaurus* was one of the last dinosaurs to live on Earth before the mass extinction event 66 million years ago at the end of the Cretaceous Period. It lived in what is now North America, along with other fan favourites such as *Triceratops* and *T. rex*!

Palaeontologists are puzzled by *Pachycephalosaurus*' teeth! It's currently believed to be a herbivore, but it also had sharp front teeth that might have been used to eat meat.

## DID YOU KNOW?

The fossilised bony domes of *Pachycephalosaurus* skulls are occasionally mistaken for dinosaur kneecaps!

*You knee-d to take a closer look!*

# TAIL TITAN

**LONGEST TAIL**

It's no surprise that the longest dinosaur tail belongs to one of the longest dinosaurs overall. Around half of *DIPLODOCUS'* total length was made up by its massive 13 to 14-m-long tail!

*Diplodocus'* long neck probably acted as a counterweight to balance out the length of its tail. At 8 m long, its neck was three times longer than the neck of a giraffe!

The vertebrae in the central part of *Diplodocus'* tail had extra bone growing underneath, which acted as support. These bones may have allowed *Diplodocus* to go onto its hind legs to reach tall plants, using its tail to help it balance.

# SAUROPOD SIBLINGS

*Diplodocus* belonged to the sauropod family of dinosaurs. Sauropods were typically large, herbivorous dinosaurs. These gentle giants walked on four legs and typically had long necks and tails, just like *Diplodocus*.

Many sauropods, including *Diplodocus*, lived and travelled together in herds.

*Diplodocus'* tail could have also been a deadly defensive weapon. It was very flexible and may have been used as a whip to lash out at predators. The loud whipping noise would have also given attackers a scare!

## 🍽 BIG APPETITE

Sauropods like *Diplodocus* had to eat a LOT of food to fuel their massive bodies. They ate all day, stripping leaves from trees with their rake-shaped teeth and munching on soft plants and ferns near the ground.

 **DID YOU KNOW?**

*Diplodocus* was nearly as long as a basketball court!

Woah, I'm massive!

# MUM'S THE WORD

**MAIASAURA** was the premier prehistoric parent! While not the only dinosaur that cared for its young, fossilised evidence suggests that *Maiasaura* went further than any other dinosaur to nurture and protect its babies.

*Maiasaura* were social animals that lived together in herds. They laid their eggs in earth nests that were grouped together for safety in numbers.

*Maiasaura* was too big and heavy to sit on its eggs to incubate them. Instead, they kept their eggs warm by covering them in rotting plants.

## 👋 BYE, BYE BABY

Not all dinosaurs were such doting parents. Many sauropod babies were pretty much self-sufficient from birth. Some palaeontologists have suggested that this was to reduce the risk of the young dinosaurs being trampled by giant grown-ups.

Fossilised bones inside *Maiasaura* eggs have revealed that newly hatched dinosaurs wouldn't have been able to walk immediately. Adult *Maiasaura* protected and brought food to their young until they could move by themselves.

## 🏆 DID YOU KNOW?

Baby *Maiasaura* were about 50 cm long but grew to their adult length of around 8 m in just seven or eight years.

*I've got a lot of growing to do!*

## 👩‍👦 MOTHER BY NAME ...

Many dinosaurs have *saurus* in their name, which is the male version of the ancient Greek word for lizard or reptile. However, due to *Maiasaura*'s nurturing nature, the female version of the same word, *saura*, was used in its name instead, along with *maia*, meaning 'good mother'.

This is a model of a *Maiasaura* nest.

# CREST CHAMPION

**LONGEST CREST**

Who needs hats when your crest makes such an impact?! Plenty of dinosaurs had crests, but none as long or impressive as **PARASAUROLOPHUS**. This dinosaur's crowning glory was its 1.8-m-long crest that curved back from its head like a massive horn.

*Parasaurolophus*' crest was hollow inside. It contained a tube that ran from its nostrils, along its crest and then looped back round at the end of the crest.

Honk! Scientists believe that *Parasaurolophus* may have blown through its crest like a trumpet to make loud noises. It may have used these sounds to warn others of danger or to communicate.

The sound waves made by *Parasaurolophus* travelled down the hollow tube in its crest, bouncing and resonating off its sides. This made the sound louder.

# CURIOUS CRESTS

*Parasaurolophus*' crest may have served several purposes. It might have also helped control its temperature, like elephants' large ears do today, or helped it clear a path through overgrown forests.

The size and shape of *Parasaurolophus* varies a bit from fossil to fossil. It may be that crest size increased with age or was different in males and females.

# QUACK, QUACK?

*Parasaurolophus* belonged to the hadrosaur family, which are often known as duck-billed dinosaurs. Despite the name, *Parasaurolophus* didn't have a flat, duck-like bill at all! Instead, it had a beak filled with teeth that it used to grind down plants.

# DID YOU KNOW?

Some scientists proposed that *Parasaurolophus*' crest might have been used as a snorkel! However, this was later shown to be impossible.

I need a snorkel, just like everyone else!

# Bonkers BIG

**BIGGEST DINOSAUR**

It's hard to imagine the massive scale of the super-sized sauropods. The biggest of them all, **PATAGOTITAN**, weighed as much as eight *T. rex* and was longer than a blue whale at 37 m long!

## Titan-ic Tribe

*Patagotitan* belonged to a family of sauropods called titanosaurs. Other contenders for the title of world's largest dinosaur include the titanosaurs *Argentinosaurus* and *Puertasaurus*. However, these dinosaurs are only known from very fragmentary remains. In some cases, only partial bones have been found, so the size of the rest of the bone has had to be estimated.

*Patagotitan*'s thigh bone measured over 2 m long. That's longer than the height of most people!

## 🌿 DINO DIGESTION

Sauropods like *Patagotitan* probably became so large because of their diet. They fed on plants that didn't contain many nutrients, and so they needed to eat a LOT of them. Digesting massive meals of plants requires a very long digestive system, and so sauropods became larger to create more space to ferment their food inside their intestines!

*Patagotitan* needed to eat about 120 kg of food per day (about the equivalent of 170 cabbages!) Luckily, they were herbivorous!

Wide hips helped to distribute *Patagotitan*'s mega weight evenly across its four, sturdy legs. They also created more tummy space for its digestive system.

In this reconstructed *Patagotitan* skeleton, you can see its set of rake-like teeth, which it used to strip leaves from branches. Its neck was flexible and could reach high into trees or swoop low to the ground to drink.

 **DID YOU KNOW?**

Although not the largest animal of all time (a title held by the blue whale!), *Patagotitan* is probably the largest animal ever to walk on Earth.

Good enough for me!

# MORE INCREDIBLE

## BEST SENSES

As well as a bone-crushing bite, **T. REX** also had super senses for tracking down its prey. Fossilised *T. rex* skulls contain an unusually large space for the part of the brain responsible for smell, which suggests that these deadly dinos had an exceptionally good sense of smell. Their orange-sized, wide-set eyes also would have given them excellent vision.

*I smell lunch!*

## MOST COLOURFUL

Fossilised pigments reveal that **CAIHONG** was covered in iridescent feathers that shimmered with lots of colours, similar to those found on hummingbirds today. *Caihong* was a small dinosaur that lived in trees, out of the reach of predators. For this reason, it didn't need brown or grey feathers as camouflage to stay safe, unlike most other prey that lived on the ground.

## LARGEST FOUND FOOTPRINTS

Palaeontologists have discovered a fossilised trail of dino footprints where each footprint measures up to **1.7 M** long. That's long enough for an average adult woman to lie down inside! The footprints were left by giant sauropods. Fossilised footprints are trace fossils - fossils created by the behaviour of living things, rather than their remains.

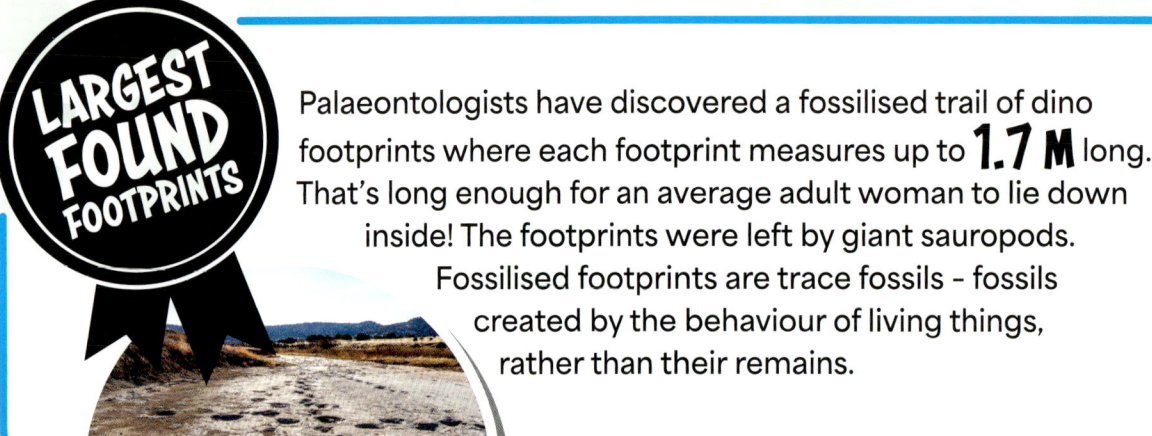

# DINOSAUR RECORDS

### LONGEST NAME

With a massive 23 letters, **MICROPACHYCEPHALOSAURUS** comes in first place! Despite the length of its name, it was actually quite a tiny dinosaur and was smaller than a cat! Its tongue-twister title means 'tiny thick-headed lizard' and comes from the ancient Greek and Latin words *micro* meaning tiny, *pachy* meaning thick, *cephalo* meaning head and *saurus* meaning lizard.

### BIGGEST EGGS

The largest dinosaur eggs measured up to 60 cm long - that's about ten times the length of a chicken egg! They were laid by large **OVIRAPTOROSAURS**, a type of theropod. Oviraptorosaurs arranged their eggs in a circle around the nest. They sat in the space in the middle so that they could incubate the eggs with their body heat without crushing them.

### LONGEST CARNIVORE

**SPINOSAURUS** measured a mega 14 m long - nearly as long as a tenpin bowling lane! It needed to eat lots of food to maintain its massive size. Palaeontologists believe it was probably semi-aquatic and hunted in and around water, like crocodiles do today. This gave it access to a wide range of prey, so it didn't go hungry!

# GLOSSARY

**carnivore** an animal that only eats meat

**cell** one of the building blocks that all living things are made up of

**diversity** having lots of different things

**era** a period of time in which the history of Earth is measured

**evolve** to change and develop gradually over time

**ferment** to go through a chemical change with the help of living things, such as bacteria

**fossil** the shape of something that has been preserved in rock for a very long time

**herbivore** an animal that only eats plants

**herd** a large group of animals that live and feed together

**mate** a reproductive partner

**palaeontologist** someone who studies dinosaurs and prehistoric life

**period** a period of time within an era

**pigment** a substance that gives something colour

**predator** an animal that kills and eats other animals for food

**prey** an animal that is killed and eaten by other animals

**reptile** a type of animal with scaly skin that lays eggs

**sauropod** a type of dinosaur with a long neck and a long tail that walked on four legs

**theropod** a type of dinosaur that walked on two legs and was often carnivorous